Beautiful Wreaths

Contributing Writers & Wreath Designers

Sylvia Montroy
Betty Valle

Publications International, Ltd.

Louis Weber, C.E.O.
Publications International, Ltd.
7373 North Cicero Avenue
Lincolnwood, Illinois 60646

ISBN 1-56173-743-7

Contributing Writers & Wreath Designers:
Sylvia Montroy is a freelance designer and member of the Society of Craft Designers. She teaches adult craft workshops and has written extensively on crafts for publications including *Better Homes and Gardens*, *Crafts Magazine*, and *Country Handcrafts*.

Betty Valle is a member and past president of the Society of Craft Designers and author of 25 craft instruction books. She has demonstrated craft projects on television and her craft designs have been published in *Redbook*, *Crafts 'N Things*, and *Crafttrends*.

Photography: Sacco Productions Limited/Chicago
   Chris Brooks
   Tom O'Connell
Photo Production: Roberta Ellis
Model: Karen Blaschek/Royal Model Management

Special acknowledgments to:
Ad-Tech™, Hampton, NH (Crafty Magic Melt Low Temp Bonder glue gun)
Aleene's Div. of Artis, Inc., Buellton, CA (all tacky glue; Right On-gloss for Welcome Wreath)

American Oak Preserving Co., Inc., North Judson, IN (glittered galaxy gyp for Paper Twist Baby Shower Wreath; rosebuds, German statice for Dried Floral Heart Swag; Spanish moss, statice sinuata, yarrow, cockscomb blossoms, globe amaranth, caspia, straw flowers for Candle Ring of Dried Flowers; Spanish moss, caspia, birch branches for Pastel Spring Wreath; cedar, boxwood, spruce, yarrow for Williamsburg-Inspired Christmas Swag)
Bleyer Industries, Inc., Valley Stream, NY (easter grass for Easter Bunny Wreath)
Cappel's Inc., Cincinnati, OH (other craft supplies)
DecoArt™, Stanford, KY (acrylic paint for Welcome Wreath; Snow-Tex™ Textural Medium for Musical Holiday Wreath)
Design Master® Color Tool, Inc., Boulder, CO (Super Surface Sealer for Herb Pinwheel Wreath and Candle Ring of Dried Flowers; Glossy Wood Tone Spray for Prize Recipe Wreath and Pine Cone Wreath; metallic spray for Victorian Wreath and Pine Cone Wreath)
Fibre-Craft® Materials Corp., Niles, IL (straw wreaths, floral pins, wire, floral tape, floral picks for most projects; cloth flowers, nylon butterflies, abaca baskets, chicks, doll hats, eggs for Easter Bunny Wreath; broom for Prize Recipe Wreath; strung beads, plastic instruments, red berries for Musical Holiday Wreath; cardinals, berries for Pine Cone Wreath; foam heart, pearl beadstring, cloth rose leaves for Simply Elegant Lace Heart Wreath)
Lion Ribbon Co., Inc., Secausus, NJ (ribbon for Candy Heart, Braided Bread Dough, Cinnamon Apple, Autumn Glow, Southwest Chili Pepper, Musical Holiday, Pine Cone, Simply Elegant Lace Heart, Pastel Spring wreaths, Dried Floral Heart Swag)
MPR Associates, Inc., High Point, NC (paper twist for Prize Recipe Wreath, Fruit & Ivy Country Wreath, Back-To-School Wreath)
Natures Medley, Charlotte, NC (potpourri for Potpourri Heart Wreath)
C.M. Offray & Son, Inc., Chester, NJ (ribbon for Batty Hattie Witch Wreath, Easter Bunny Wreath, Victorian Wreath, Fruit & Ivy Country Wreath)
Plaid Enterprises, Norcross, GA (Treasure Crystal Cote for Braided Bread Dough Wreath; paper twist for Paper Twist Baby Shower Wreath)
St. Louis Trimming, Inc., St. Louis, MO (ruffled lace for Simply Elegant Lace Heart Wreath)

CONTENTS

INTRODUCTION

———— ❧ ————

For many of us, home decor is high on our list of priorities. Whether we have a house or an apartment, our ultimate goal is to create a pleasant, comfortable atmosphere for everyday living.

The visual impact you can add to each room in your home is at your fingertips, and what better place to start than by making your own handcrafted wreaths from the wide selection in this book? There are wreaths to choose from for every season, for most holidays, and for special occasions. Complete them for your use or give them as gifts; experience the satisfaction of having made them yourself.

As you leaf through these pages, notice the clearly photographed, step-by-step instructions that will help you to carry out each design. The introduction is packed with valuable information—from a descriptive list of tools and floral aids to selecting wreath bases and ribbon. Have you always wanted to make a pretty bow? Check out the section on bow making. There is even a segment on "Designing Tips." Spread your wings and develop your own original designs! With a little perseverance and lots of pride in your work, you will soon be creating your own beautiful wreaths.

TOOLS AND FLORAL AIDS

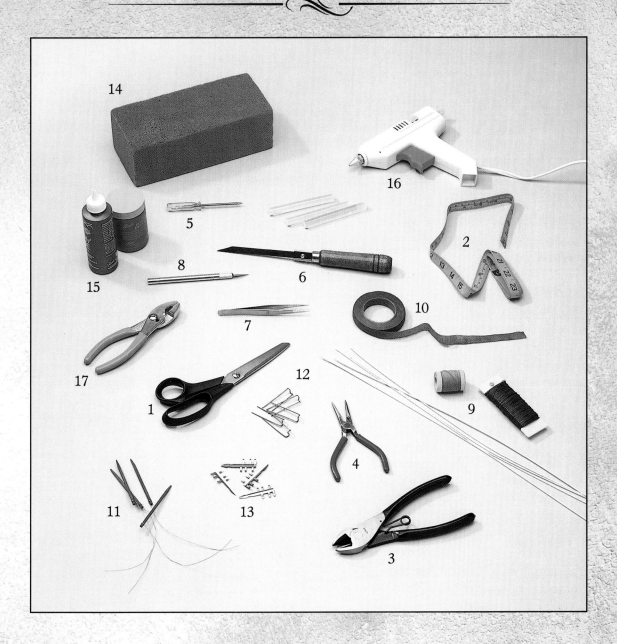

As you begin your wreath-making venture, there are basic tools and floral aids you should be familiar with. Some you may already own, while others you may have to buy.

1. **Scissors** should be sharp and are used mainly for cutting ribbon, fabric, and lace. Keep them handy; you'll reach for them often.

2. A **tape measure** will help you in countless ways, from measuring ribbon to determining the height or width of your design.

3. **Wire cutters** are used to cut wire stems, floral wire, and other objects that cannot be cut by scissors. They will also snip small branches and the stems of dried flowers. You could also use small **garden clippers** for many of the same jobs, though these may be needed for heavier jobs, such as cutting heavy branches.

4. **Needle-nosed pliers** are used to grasp materials that your fingers cannot. They are also helpful when twisting heavier gauge wire. This is an all-purpose tool.

5. An **awl** resembles an ice pick and can be used to make a hole in a straw wreath or into artificial fruit that requires the attachment of a wooden pick.

6. A **serrated knife**, or steak knife, is used to cut and shape floral and plastic foam.

7. **Tweezers** are occasionally needed to handle small items.

8. A **small craft knife** is not an essential tool, but it may come in handy. It can be used in place of scissors to cut materials, such as corrugated cardboard.

9. **Floral wire** comes in many gauges. The higher the gauge number, the finer the wire. Wire hangers can be fashioned from 16-gauge wire, while 18- and 20-gauge wire are used to strengthen flower stems. The finer gauges, from 28 to 32 gauge, can be used for making bows.

Wire is sold in 12" and 18" straight lengths as well as on spools and paddles. If it is to be used for stems, straight lengths are best. Wrap the finer spool or paddle wire around preserved or dried materials when attaching them to a wreath or garland.

Cloth-covered wire is available in several colors and gauges and serves many purposes. When securing the gathers of a bow, 30- or 32-gauge wire that matches the ribbon is easily camouflaged. This wire comes in one yard lengths and on spools.

10. **Floral tape** is a waxy crepe paper that will stick only to itself when stretched. It is available in many colors. Choose the shade closest to the materials you are working with, you may need several different colors, and use it to cover stems and to reinforce wired floral picks.

11. **Wired floral picks** are made of wood and come in several lengths. Use them to reinforce or lengthen stems that are to be inserted in floral and plastic foam or into a straw wreath.

12. **Greening** or **fern pins** are U-shaped pins. They are also known as **pole, craft,** or **floral pins.** Use them to attach materials to foam or straw wreaths. We have called them floral pins throughout this book.

13. **Steel floral picks,** made for a florist's pick machine, can be used manually by attaching the pick to the flower stem and squeezing the prongs around the stem with pliers.

14. **Dry floral foam,** made specifically for dried or silk flowers, is strong enough to hold the stems yet soft enough to allow penetration without wire or pick reinforcement. Do not confuse it with wet floral foam, which is designed to absorb water while keeping fresh flowers alive. Although this latter type may work for some florals, it usually crumbles and the materials will loosen and can fall out.

15. **Craft glue** ranges in consistency from thick to thin. You usually have to wait between steps for the glue to dry. Always have some on hand and select those that dry clear.

16. **Glue guns** are one of the most timesaving of all craft tools. There are guns for hot glue, low temperature glue, and those that dispense either type at the flip of a switch. There is no need to wait between steps because the glue sets up in seconds. NOTE: *When selecting a gun that requires its own special glue, be sure you have a source for the purchase of additional glue.*

Hot glue guns melt glue at up to 380° and can cause severe burns. They are not recommended for use by children, but they are useful. If used correctly, their advantages far outweigh this one disadvantage.

Low temperature glue guns dispense glue at a much lower temperature. The chances of being burned are slim. Avoid hanging your wreath outdoors where the hot sun could melt the glue, which would loosen the materials. Low temperature glue is ideal for indoor use, and you can glue plastic and floral foam without melting it.

Regardless of which glue gun you use, work quickly once you've applied the melted glue. The glue looses its adhesiveness as it cools. Hold the glued object in place for a few seconds while the glue cools and adheres. Fine webs of glue will hang from your completed wreath. Remove them with tweezers from fragile dried materials. From sturdy materials, such as pine cone wreaths, a hand-held hair dryer will melt them away.

17. **Pliers** are used to manually attach steel floral picks to dried stems.

WREATH BASES

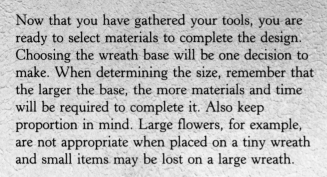

Now that you have gathered your tools, you are ready to select materials to complete the design. Choosing the wreath base will be one decision to make. When determining the size, remember that the larger the base, the more materials and time will be required to complete it. Also keep proportion in mind. Large flowers, for example, are not appropriate when placed on a tiny wreath and small items may be lost on a large wreath.

The choice of wreath bases is endless, and each type offers a variety of shapes. From round, to hearts, to basket-shaped, to arches, these bases will often dictate the type of design. **Straw wreaths** and those made of **grapevines** or **twigs** are attractive, and when left partially exposed will add to the design. Conversely, **plastic foam** and **wire bases** must be completely concealed, which requires an all-over design and more materials. In addition to those mentioned, **excelsior** and **willow wreaths** are also exciting options.

RIBBON

Ribbon plays an important role in wreath design. When selecting it for your project, consideration should be given to the theme and style of the wreath. An informal wreath should sport a casual ribbon, while a more sophisticated wreath will be enhanced by something elegant. Choose colors and styles to complement your home decor.

Ribbons are sold in many widths, and using more than one width of coordinated ribbons on the same wreath will add a lovely accent. Ribbons range from velvet and polyester to cotton and satin. For elegance, there are metallics and laces. Wire-edge ribbons allow you to shape your bows in a unique fashion. The versatility of paper ribbon, both twisted and flat, is astounding. New and exciting paper products are constantly being introduced. With all of these choices, it becomes a challenge to select your favorite. Let your imagination lead you!

NATURAL MATERIALS

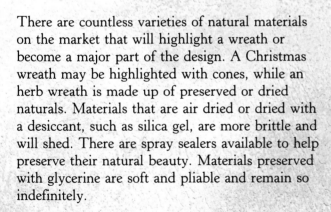

There are countless varieties of natural materials on the market that will highlight a wreath or become a major part of the design. A Christmas wreath may be highlighted with cones, while an herb wreath is made up of preserved or dried naturals. Materials that are air dried or dried with a desiccant, such as silica gel, are more brittle and will shed. There are spray sealers available to help preserve their natural beauty. Materials preserved with glycerine are soft and pliable and remain so indefinitely.

The texture and beauty of mosses should not be overlooked. Whether you cover the entire wreath or glue tiny accent pieces at random, the design is enhanced by its use. Spanish moss, found hanging from trees in the southern U.S. and in tropical America, is a light feathery gray moss commonly used in making wreaths. Commercially processed, it is free of insects. Lovely green mosses, such as

sheet moss and spaghnum, will add texture and color to your wreath. Another option is a commercially made thin plastic sheet that is flocked with a layer of fine green moss. It is pliable, easy to work with, and lends itself well to small florals.

Don't forget the versatility of cones and pods, whether you make an entire wreath of them or use them as embellishments. Acorns, magnolia pods, sweet gum balls, casuarina pods, and cones of every size and description grow in the wild. If you choose to collect your own, it is best to get permission from the property owner. Be aware that it is illegal to gather wild materials on some public lands. After collecting your items, bake them in a 150° oven for no more than one hour, which eliminates insects and eggs. Avoid overbaking. If properly stored, cones and pods will last indefinitely.

HOW-TO FLORAL PROCEDURES

This section explains how to perform several of the steps necessary to complete designs in this book.

HANGING A WREATH

Chenille stem or **pipe cleaner hanger:** Use only on wreaths covered with materials that will conceal this hanger. Bend a 12" length evenly into a *U*. Twist the *U* end into a 1" or 2" oval loop. Wrap and twist the ends around the wreath tightly, positioning the loop at the top. VARIATION: Use the same technique to wrap the chenille stem tightly around a wire ring or grapevine wreath, far enough down on the back so it is not visible from the front. You can also use this technique with wired paper twist.

Wire-loop hanger: Use only on straw or plastic foam wreaths. Bend 6" of heavy floral wire into a *U*. Twist the *U* end into a 1" oval loop. Bend the cut ends at right angles to the loop and push them into the foam or straw until the loop is flush with the wreath. Secure to the wreath with hot glue placed on the twisted end of the hanger.

FLORAL TAPE

Floral tape will stick only to itself when stretched. To apply it, either break off a length or hook the roll of tape over your little finger. Stretch and wrap it around the stem diagonally. Overlap the tape, allowing it to stick to itself, and break it off at the end.

FLORAL PICKS

Use wired floral picks to lengthen or strengthen weak stems when inserting them into plastic foam, floral foam, or straw. Attach them by overlapping the wired end of the pick with about 1" of the stem end. Spiral wrap the wire tightly around both, working down one inch. Continue wrapping one time around the pick itself, and then back up with the rest of the wire. This helps lock the two together.

As reinforcement, stretch and wrap floral tape on the wired area only. To tape the entire pick may cause friction when inserting it into foam or straw.

LOCK-WRAP STEMS

This method is used to lengthen and reinforce stems while locking the wire and stem together. Wrap about 1" of the stem tightly with floral tape. Lay the floral wire parallel to the stem with the top of the wire even with the top of the wrapped tape. Leaving the top of the wire exposed, wrap the wire and stem together for several inches with tape. Break the tape. With needle-nosed pliers, bend the wire at the top of the stem down flush against the taped stem. Wrap the entire stem with tape, from the bent wire to the bottom.

COVERING A STRAW OR PLASTIC FOAM WREATH

When using Spanish moss: Loosen the Spanish moss and discard tiny twigs. Spread moss evenly on all sides of the wreath and secure with floral pins. Wrap clear monofilament (fishing) line or matching thread around the moss to keep it intact. As you begin wrapping, tie a knot, leaving a 12" length of line hanging. Continue to spiral the long end and use the 12" length to tie off both ends when you finish. With scissors, cut the excess line and trim the stray ends of moss neatly. NOTE: *This same procedure can be used to cover a wreath with Easter grass, excelsior, or similar materials.*

MAKING BOWS

There are many ways to make bows, and the more you make, the easier it becomes. We have given you a number of choices. Follow the instructions, and before long you will be a pro.

To make your bows more professional, here are two ways to cut ribbon ends:

To *V-cut* ribbon, gently fold the ribbon ends in half lengthwise. Cut from the outside edge up 1½" toward the fold.

To angle-cut ribbon, cut the ends at an angle in either direction.

French bow from paper twist

1. With wire cutters, cut the twisted paper into four lengths: 21", 17", 13", and 6". Untwist the paper, but do not spread it to its full width. From the three largest lengths, make three individual circles by overlapping each 2" and hot gluing. In the same manner, make a knot from the 6" length by overlapping the ends 1", creating a small circle.

2. Stack and glue graduated loops on top of each other, ending with the knot on top (make sure seams are to back of bow). Crimp the centers as you glue. Use floral wire to tighten and hold bow together. To conceal the glued centers, you can insert a 5" strip of untwisted ribbon through the knot. Glue the ends together on the back.

3. To make a streamer, untwist a 14" length of paper twist. Crimp in the middle to form an inverted V. Secure to bow by twisting wire around crimped center of streamer. (If you are putting a bow directly onto a wreath, you can also secure the streamer to a wreath with a floral pin. Glue the bow over the streamer to conceal the pin.) You can V-cut or angle-cut the streamer ends.

INTRODUCTION

E-Z bow

1. This bow is added directly to a wreath. Cut the desired number of ribbon lengths to make the streamers. Angle- or V-cut streamer ends. Crimp the streamers in the middle and attach to the wreath with a floral pin.

2. Cut the desired number of ribbons to make individual clustered loops; angle- or V-cut the ends of each. To make one cluster, fold the end of one strip over 6" with wrong sides together. Crimp the ribbon midway at 3" and continue folding and crimping, making two loops and one end on each side. Place a floral pin over the crimped center and attach to the wreath above the streamer.

3. Place the individual clusters in a tight group. Fluff the loops to conceal the pins.

Multiloop bow

1. Crimp the ribbon between thumb and forefinger at the desired streamer length, with the streamer hanging down. Make an equal number of loops on each side of your thumb by crimping each individually while you guide the ribbon into a loop in a circular direction. Crimp each new loop next to the previous one, rather than on top. Secure the loops in the center with wire twisted tightly on the back, leaving the second streamer pointing up.

2. While holding the bow in the same position, roll 3" of that streamer toward you over your thumb, making a small center loop as a knot. If the ribbon has a right and wrong side, twist the loop right side out and catch the loop under your thumb. The streamer will again be pointing up. Bring one end of wire from the back over that streamer beside the knot and to the back again. Twist the wires. Bring the streamers beneath the bow and V- or angle-cut the ends.

Shoestring bow

This is an alternative to a hand-tied shoestring bow. To make a small bow, glue a toothpick or 1/8" wooden dowel vertically into a 2" x 4" x 2" tall scrap of plastic foam. Bring the ribbon ends around the dowel to the front. Tie the bow loops immediately, eliminating the first knot usually made when tying a shoe. Slip the bow off the dowel. Tighten and shape it. Angle-cut the streamer ends.

DESIGNING TIPS

We have created these wreath designs for you and encourage you to duplicate them. We also urge you to develop your own designs. Here are a few suggestions to help stimulate your creativity:

Study wreaths in books, magazines, and even mail order catalogs; analyze those designs. Determine what you like, don't like, and why. Look at color combinations, and how ribbons and florals are arranged. Don't underestimate your own ability to evaluate design objectively. After a time, you will develop your own style that will grow and change as you become more experienced in creating your own wreaths.

As you study various wreaths, notice that your eyes may be drawn to an area of particular interest. It should be pleasing to look at, and it could convey the message of the theme. It is the "focal point" of that wreath. Not all wreaths must have a focal point, but those that do will draw the viewer's attention.

If you can't decide where to begin, start by choosing a theme—a special holiday or season of the year, perhaps. With the wide variety of ribbons available today, you might want to select a ribbon pattern that strikes your fancy. Pick up those ribbon colors in floral accessories for the wreath. Use the ribbon as a springboard for the rest of the design and let your creativity flow. You could take the same approach using flowers as your inspiration and build from there.

After you have chosen a theme and acquired your materials, sketch your design. But do not let your sketch prevent you from changing plans once you've begun. Allow yourself flexibility. An alternative is to attach the materials to the wreath temporarily with T-pins or floral pins, if the design is not too intricate. You may also loosely wire them on. Change the arrangement of materials until something suits you. Leave it for several hours or overnight. Then study it again as though you were seeing it for the first time. If you don't like something, change it. When satisfied, assemble the wreath permanently.

For the best perspective, always try to arrange your wreath in a hanging position. If that is not possible, view it upright between steps. Study it from a distance, or better yet, look at it in a mirror. If materials aren't balanced, appear overpowering, or are crowded, the reflection should tell you that.

If this is your first experience with making a wreath, you may not be aware of the infinite choice of accessories at your disposal. Visit your local floral and craft stores and acquaint yourself with the market. Here are a few suggestions:

There are colorful feathered birds as well as birdhouses, nests, and eggs that all fit in well with spring and summer themes, not to mention autumn and Christmas. In addition, holiday and seasonal ornaments could find a place in your designing. Wood shapes of animals, buildings, and words of greeting can become the focal point of your wreath. An assortment of brooms, hats, and baskets give personality to stuffed animals.

At home, you may already have a collection of old costume jewelry that could be the key to an exquisite wreath. Everyday items such as sewing notions, small toys, and stationery supplies can develop into a special theme. Whether they are fresh or artificial, fruits and vegetables form the basis of a savory culinary wreath. Tucked away in a closet or drawer may be the components for a unique wreath. Do you have cones or sea shells collected while on vacation? Perhaps the shells will inspire a nautical wreath. If you are a gardener, perhaps you have bright new gardening gloves to which you can add a terra cotta pot, a shiny trowel, and other related materials. If a design plan does not evolve immediately, do not be discouraged. Keep your goal in mind, and when you least expect it the idea could surface.

We have unlocked the gate leading to a new creative adventure for you, and you have stepped inside. Now, follow the path to develop your own personal style of design and enjoy your accomplishments.

HERB PINWHEEL WREATH

A classic wreath of fragrant dried herbs placed pinwheel fashion creates a design of delicate beauty. A variety of herbs give delicate color and scent to this wreath. Perhaps you could include some herbs from your own garden. The natural beauty of this wreath will enhance any area where it is displayed.

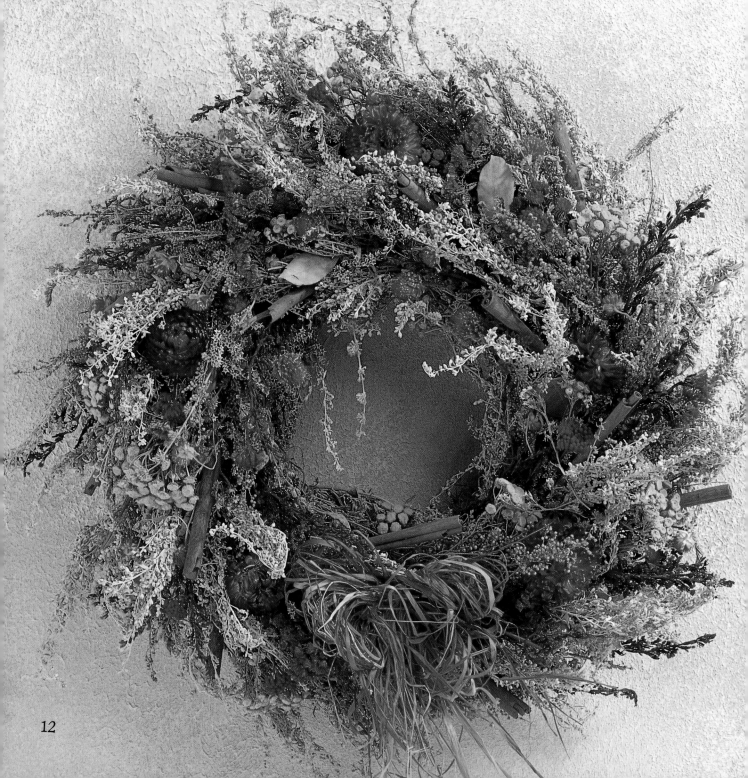

1. Lay straw wreath in bed of Spanish moss. Bring moss around wreath to cover. Secure moss with floral pins. Wrap gray carpet thread around wreath to hold moss in place. Use a piece of raffia to make a chenille stem hanger (see page 8).

2. Lay stem of small cluster of German statice on prongs of steel floral pick. Bend prongs around stems with pliers. Make 30 picks. (Note: Steel picks may be used in pick machine if you have one.) Pick statice into wreath distributing evenly over wreath surface. Direct all materials in the same direction.

3. Repeat process for 30 7" to 8" long clusters of artemisia.

Materials

- 10" straw wreath
- Spanish moss, approx. ½ lb.
- floral pins
- gray carpet thread
- German statice, approx. 30 clusters (6" long)
- steel floral picks
- pliers
- artemisia, approx. 30 clusters (7" to 8" long)
- tacky glue
- 1 pkg. dried pennyroyal
- 1 bunch dried sweet Anne
- 1 bunch dried heather
- 10 to 12 cinnamon sticks (6" long)
- 1 bunch tansy
- 1 pkg. dried globe amaranth, purple
- dried bay leaves
- statice sinuata, purple
- straw flowers, burgundy
- burgundy and mauve raffia
- surface sealer

4. Dip stems of all other materials into tacky glue and place into wreath. Place pennyroyal, sweet Anne, heather, and cinnamon sticks first. Then place tansy, globe amaranth, bay leaves, statice sinuata, and straw flowers.

5. Shred 3 or 4 strands of both burgundy and mauve raffia with a straight pin. Form shredded raffia into bow shape (6" wide, with 6" streamers) and tie in center with a strand of raffia. Slip floral pin through center of raffia strand, dip end of pin into glue, then push into bottom of wreath. Spray wreath with surface sealer to protect dried materials from shattering.

CANDY HEART WREATH

Pretty wrapped candies in a heart-shaped wreath set the mood for a sweet Valentine. A warm and loving welcome is expressed with your thoughtfulness when you place this luscious wreath on your door to share a sweet treat with visitors.

Materials

- 1 strong wire coat hanger
  (Do not use lightweight shirt
  hangers)
- 4 lbs. (approx.) of wrapped
  hard candy
- 28-gauge spool wire
- wire cutters
- 1⅓ yards red satin ribbon
- 1½ yards white lace with red
  satin ribbon
- scissors
- 1 child's scissors
- glue gun and glue sticks
- bleached, preserved galaxy
  gypsophila (gyp), 3 or 4
  sprigs

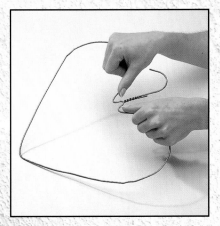

1. Shape coat hanger into circle, working out kinks in the wire. Bend down hanger to form deep indent in heart and form point on bottom of circle to form bottom of heart. Bend down hook and form hanger with pliers.

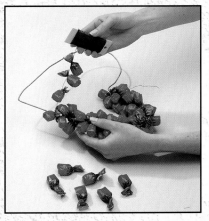

2. Wrap spool wire around one end of wrapped candy several times, pulling wire very tight. Repeat for several more pieces of candy, spacing candy about 1" to 2" apart. Wrap end of wire around heart to secure, then wrap wire with candy around heart. Keep adding candy and wrapping until heart is filled with candy. Pull wire tight and twist ends together.

3. Cut off 12" of satin ribbon and tie around indent of heart. Work ribbon into candy so that it doesn't show. This will keep the indent from giving under weight of candy.

4. Using lace ribbon, make 6 loop bow with no center loop (5" wide, with 12" streamers). Attach one yard of red satin ribbon to back of bow with bow wire. Apply glue to the back of bow and place bow to left side of wreath, bringing bow wire to back of wreath. Pull wire tight and twist ends together. Trim excess wire. Tie scissors onto satin ribbon (make sure satin ribbon is long enough to reach other side of heart).

5. Cluster together 5 pieces of candy with wire. Pull wire tight and twist together to secure. Place glue into center of bow and rest candy cluster into glue, bring wire ends to back of wreath. Twist ends together and trim excess wire. Apply glue to stems of sprigs of gyp and place into candy cluster.

PAPER TWIST BABY
SHOWER WREATH

Puffs of white paper twist give a billowy, cloudlike appearance and provide a soft background for baby trinkets and toys. A soft bow of blue and pink paper twist and a cascade of colored plastic safety pin rattles complement the wreath. A lovely decoration for a shower, which can then be given to the mother-to-be for the nursery.

1. Make a chenille stem hanger (see page 8). Untwist all paper twist. Beginning on outside edge of wreath, pin end of white twist to wreath with floral pin. Loop about 6" length of twist and pin into wreath again about 2" from starting point. Continue around outside edge. Then repeat same process for top and inside edge of wreath.

2. Using blue paper twist, make 4 loop bow (10" wide, with 10" streamers). Add 2 loop pink bow in center of blue bow. Tie ribbons to plastic safety pins of corresponding color. Arrange ribbons so safety pins fall at staggered lengths. Attach ribbons to bow wire in back of bow. Wire bow to left side of wreath.

3. Wrap wire around neck of teddy bear, dip ends of wire into glue and insert into foam. (Change ribbon color around teddy's neck to pink.)

4. Dip stems of mini mums into glue and insert stems into foam, clustering several together. Dip stems of glittered gyp into glue and insert into wreath.

5. Attach wire to each baby toy and glue into foam. Add pink or blue ⅛" bow to each toy if desired.

Materials

- 14" extruded foam wreath
- white chenille stem for hanger
- 12 yards 7½" white paper twist
- floral pins
- 1½ yards 4" blue paper twist
- 1½ yards 4" pink paper twist
- ⅛" satin ribbon: ½ yard blue and yellow, 2 yards pink
- scissors
- 3 safety pin rattles
- 6" plush teddy bear
- 18-gauge white covered wire
- wire cutters
- tacky glue
- silk mini mums (8 each of pink, blue, yellow)
- preserved, bleached, glittered galaxy gypsophila (gyp)
- assorted baby toys

DRIED FLORAL
HEART SWAG

Velvet ribbon forms the base for this lovely dried swag, accented with tiny twig hearts, German statice, and rosebuds. Wire-edge metallic gold ribbon shapes the perky bows that blend with the brass ring hanger. Try changing the color of the ribbon and rosebuds to match your home decor!

Materials

- 1 yard red velvet craft ribbon, 2½" wide
- 1 yard white scalloped edge lace ribbon, 1½" wide
- tape measure
- scissors
- glue gun and glue sticks
- 29" of ⅛" wooden dowel
- tacky glue
- toothpick
- wire cutters
- 2" diameter gold ring
- three 4" twig hearts
- approx. 26 natural German statice sprigs
- 5 dried red rosebuds
- 2 yards wire-edge metallic gold ribbon, ⅝" wide

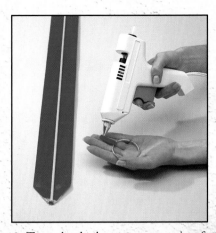

1. Cut 30" length from both red velvet and lace ribbon. Glue lace ribbon centered on plush side of the velvet ribbon; use hot glue sparingly. Trim ends of both ribbons evenly. Cut a V in bottom by gently folding ribbon in half lengthwise and cut at an angle, about 1½" toward the fold.

2. For stability, glue the wood dowel to the center back of the swag by spreading tacky glue on the dowel with a toothpick. Trim dowel to fit, using wire cutters. Fold top ends of swag back to form two triangles (meeting at dowel). Allow the glue to dry.

3. To make the hanger, cut a strip of velvet ribbon, ¼"×2¾". Put the ribbon through the brass ring and hot glue the ends together. Hot glue those ribbon ends to the dowel on the upper back, allowing only the ring to show from the front.

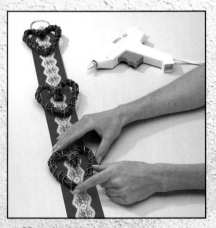

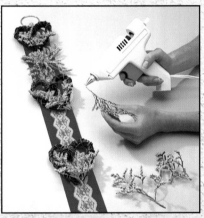

4. Hot glue three twig heart wreaths to the front of the swag: the first (upper) heart is 1" from the top; the second heart is 10" from the top; the third heart is 19" from the top. There will be 7" at the bottom of the ribbon.

5. At the lower points of each heart and extending up each side, hot glue a 2" to 3" sprig of statice with the stems converging at the point. Leave upper half of each heart uncovered. Glue shorter statice sprigs to fill in. Glue additional statice sprigs to the lace between all hearts and beneath the third heart to the bottom of the swag. Overlap each sprig to conceal the glued stems.

6. Hot glue three rosebuds in a cluster at the lower point of the second heart. Glue one rosebud to each point of the first and third hearts. Cut three 24" lengths of metallic ribbon; make three shoestring bows. Cut each streamer at an angle and gently curl each around your finger. Hot glue a bow to the statice about 2" below each heart.

PRIZE RECIPE WREATH

Feature your cherished family recipe on this novel kitchen wreath as a reminder of fond memories. Accent it with wooden utensils and fruit.

Materials

- 14" straw wreath
- wire cutters
- 6" 16-gauge wire
- glue gun and glue sticks
- scissors
- tape measure
- 3½ yards green paper twist
- 2 floral pins
- 12" flat pine or straw broom
- 1" diameter artificial fruit: 3 apples, 3 lemons, 3 pears (preferably on picks with green cloth leaves)
- 12 2" green cloth leaves, any variety (if not included with fruit)
- 3½" to 4½" miniature wooden utensils: fork, spoon, cutting board, rolling pin (or those of your choice)
- red acrylic paint
- small art brush
- 5" square cardboard
- 8½" × 11" sheet off-white stationery
- copy machine
- wood tone spray
- pencil

1. Following instructions on page 8, make a wire-loop hanger and glue it to the upper back of the wreath. With scissors, neatly trim the stray ends of straw from the wreath. With wire cutters, cut 62" of paper twist. Untwist but don't spread it to its full width. Spiral it evenly around the wreath, bring the ends together on the back and secure with a floral pin. Glue the broom handle to the wreath at the top, just left of center so it falls diagonally.

2. Make a French bow from the remaining paper twist (see page 9). Glue it to the handle to fall horizontally on the wreath. If the fruit is wired, cut the wires off and glue a cluster of four leaves and three different fruits under the bow in the center just below the handle. Glue the remaining leaves and fruit in a cluster centered at the base of the broom, leaving room to attach the wooden utensils. Glue three different utensils in a fan shape to the wreath below the fruit cluster.

3. Paint the rolling pin handles red and allow to dry. To determine the size to make your recipe, measure the space left on the front of the broom. On the wreath pictured, a recipe 4" × 4¾" was used. Cut a piece of cardboard as a guide. On a copy machine and on copy paper, reduce the recipe to fit within your cardboard boundary, then copy the recipe onto stationery. Place cardboard pattern on the back of the stationery, centering it behind the recipe. Draw around the cardboard on the back. Use those lines to fold and tear a jagged edge.

4. In a well-ventilated area, lightly spray both sides of the recipe with the spray. Curl and glue the upper left corner forward over the rolling pin. Roll the lower right corner forward over a pencil. Remove the pencil and glue the rolled paper in place. Glue the rolled corners of the recipe to the broom, arranging a ripple across the paper.

WELCOME WREATH

A grapevine wreath is lovely to display outdoors. A friendly welcome
is conveyed by the wild flower and ivy arrangement.

1. Using wired paper twist, attach hanger (see page 8). Wrap two lengths of wired paper twist across bottom half of wreath, twisting ends in back. Loosely weave twist in and out of these and wreath branches to form a loose basket.

2. Line basket with layer of Spanish moss. Place brick foam into moss in basket. Run length of wired paper twist through bottom of basket and bring around foam to secure foam into basket. Cover top of foam with Spanish moss and secure with floral pins.

3. Dip stems of flowers into tacky glue before inserting into foam. Add English ivy into basket area. Cut sprays apart for better distribution. Use 3 sprays in basket and glue remaining ivy sprigs into vine around wreath. Place one spray of peach blossoms to left of center, with blossoms reaching the bottom edge of top of wreath. Divide second blossom spray and place one sprig left and one cascading down from left of center. Place azaleas in center. Pink blush rosebuds are clustered to right of center and mini bright pink rosebuds and baby breath are used to fill arrangement.

Materials

- 20" grapevine wreath
- 6 yards wired paper twist, natural
- wire cutters
- Spanish moss
- 1 brick dry floral foam
- floral pins
- tacky glue
- 5 silk English ivy sprays, 24" long, 3 branches each
- 3 silk blossom sprays, peach
- 2 silk azalea sprays, 6 blossoms, medium yellow
- 3 silk dried-look rosebuds, pink blush
- 2 silk dried-look mini rosebud sprays, deep pink
- 2 silk dried-look baby breath sprays, candlelight
- blue feather butterfly, 3½"
- 2 yards floral chintz ribbon
- 28-gauge white-covered wire
- 3" wood floral pick
- 1 wooden welcome, 10" × 2"
- acrylic paint, buttermilk and light avocado
- ¼" paintbrush
- water base varnish

4. Place butterfly on wire stem right of center among rosebuds and azaleas. Make 6 loop bow from chintz ribbon (9" wide, with 8" streamers) and attach to 3" wood floral pick. Dip floral pick into glue and push into floral foam at center front of wreath.

5. Paint welcome sign with buttermilk acrylic paint (2 coats). When dry, dip brush into water then into light avocado paint. Brush paint across welcome sign and immediately wipe away excess paint for an antiqued look. Let dry, then give several coats of water base varnish. Glue sign to top of wreath. (It may be necessary to wire sign to wreath.)

EASTER BUNNY WREATH

This whimsical wreath renews our fond childhood memories of that busy little rabbit who accomplished a monumental task while we slept. Delight the youngsters in your life by covering a straw wreath with Easter grass; add a bunny and Easter ornaments.

1. Make a wire loop hanger (see page 8). Cut a small section from the plastic wrap on the upper back of the wreath and glue on the hanger. Leave the remaining plastic wrap intact. Cover the wreath with Easter grass, attach with floral pins, and wrap with fishing line. Make a multiloop bow (see page 10) measuring 8" across, with 9" and 10" streamers. Glue bow to the bottom middle of the wreath.

2. Glue 12 cloth flowers in a cluster to the rabbit's head in front of her ears. Tie a shoestring bow and glue it under her chin. Glue a butterfly to her left ear and right front paw.

3. Cut a wooden dowel (with wire cutters) the height of the rabbit's head and body plus 2". Glue the dowel vertically to the back of the head and body with the 2" extending beneath the body. If necessary, use an awl to ream a hole in the straw above the bow. Push the dowel into the straw at the center bottom of the wreath.

4. To make an Easter basket of eggs, wad a small amount of leftover Easter grass and glue it inside the basket. Trim the stray grass. Apply glue to the basket and grass and embed four eggs into the glue. Glue the basket to the rabbit's left front paw. Make six more Easter baskets of eggs and glue them to the wreath at various angles. Make certain to glue some to the outside edges and also the inside edge near the rabbit.

5. Glue the chicks and hats, evenly distributing the variety and colors. Place a small puddle of glue in the grass and embed a cluster of five eggs into the glue. Glue seven egg clusters evenly around the wreath.

Materials

- 14" plastic wrapped straw wreath
- 6" 16-gauge wire
- wire cutters
- glue gun and glue sticks
- 4 oz. pink Easter grass
- 30 floral pins
- scissors
- 8 yards clear monofilament fishing line or pink thread
- tape measure
- 2⅓ yards cotton print ribbon
- 6" 32-gauge white cloth-covered wire
- 7" plush stuffed sitting rabbit
- 12 2" cloth flowers
- 2 1" yellow nylon butterflies
- 12" ⅛" rose ribbon
- ¹⁄₁₆" wood dowel
- awl
- 7 1¾" abaca baskets
- 63 ½" pastel Easter eggs
- 6 1¼" flocked yellow chicks
- 4 1¼" assorted doll hats

PASTEL SPRING WREATH

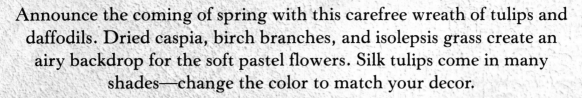

Announce the coming of spring with this carefree wreath of tulips and daffodils. Dried caspia, birch branches, and isolepsis grass create an airy backdrop for the soft pastel flowers. Silk tulips come in many shades—change the color to match your decor.

Materials

- 14" round straw wreath
- wire cutters
- 6" 16-gauge wire
- glue gun and glue sticks
- scissors
- tape measure
- 14 floral pins
- 8 yards rose cotton print ribbon
- 20 2½" wired floral picks
- green floral tape
- needle-nosed pliers
- awl
- 2 clusters green isolepsis grass
- 20 18" fine tips of birch branches (with several attached to a main branch)
- 7 14" branches of natural dried caspia
- silk flowers with leaves on 12" stems: 4 rose or pink tulips, 3 white daffodils
- sundrop yellow spray paint (optional)
- 1 oz. Spanish moss

1. Make a wire-loop hanger (see page 8); glue it to the top back of wreath. Trim stray straw ends from wreath. Spiral about 2 yards of ribbon evenly around the wreath, bringing the ends together on the back with a floral pin. Leave the bottom center of wreath free of ribbon to insert florals.

2. Attach floral picks to materials (see page 8) as needed. When inserting florals, angle stems to converge at bottom. With needle-nosed pliers, grasp the pick and insert isolepsis grass in the center, extreme back of the wreath. If necessary, use an awl to make a hole in the straw. Separate blades of grass to fall in a fan.

3. Insert three tall birch branches with fine tips around the grass in a fan shape, permitting some wispy tips to extend 6" to 8" above the wreath. Use wire cutters to clip the branches when necessary. Attach three stems of caspia in a fan shape, one in the center extending 14" from stem to tip and two on each side 12" tall.

4. When attaching tulips to picks, measure from cut stem end to tip as follows: two 10", one 8", and one 6". Remove tulip leaves and reserve. With needle-nosed pliers and an awl, insert one 10" tulip vertically in line with top of wreath. Angle the remaining 10" tulip to fall to the left of the top. Angle the 8" tulip toward the right side, and the 6" farther toward the right.

5. Attach picks to 9", 6", and 5" daffodils. Leave the daffodil leaves attached but slide them up the stem toward the blossom. If desired, spray the flower centers with sundrop yellow. Insert the daffodils in a cluster at various levels.

6. Attach picks to three leaves and insert around the daffodils to cascade over the edge. Glue stems of caspia to fill in spaces among the flowers, keeping within the shape of the wreath.

7. Cut four 33" ribbons for bows. Cut two 24" and one 30" streamers. Crimp streamers in the middle. Place the 24" ones on top of the 30" one. Attach them to bottom of wreath with a floral pin. Position them in a fan shape with the longest in the center and the shorter ones on the outside.

8. Cut a V on the ends of the streamers at different levels. Spot glue streamers to the adjoining streamer as close to the wreath as possible. Ripple the two outside streamers by spot gluing each to the adjoining streamer twice. Make an E-Z bow with remaining ribbon (see page 10), making four separate loop clusters.

9. Glue about six fine birch tips behind the bow on each side, to extend 7" to 9" horizontally from bow's center. Glue caspia stems over the birch, filling in with shorter sprigs of caspia.

10. Loosen Spanish moss and lightly pack around the bow to conceal the glued branches; attach moss with floral pins.

POTPOURRI HEART
WREATH

Fragrant fabric hearts trimmed with lace, ribbons, and flowers are pinned onto a lace covered wreath base. This versatile wreath is embellished with a lovely silk flower nosegay and a loopy lace bow. The hearts may be removed and given to guests as a bridal shower favor or for afternoon bridge favors. Make an extra set of hearts and give the wreath to the bride-to-be for her new home.

Materials

- flat foam wreath, 12" × 1½" × 1"
- 5 yards French blue moire ribbon
- glue, either cool temp glue gun and clear sticks or tacky glue
- scissors
- 8 yards 3" wide eggshell lace ribbon
- 28-gauge white-covered wire
- wire cutters
- hand stapler and staples
- tracing paper and pencil
- ¼ yard small pink and blue floral print fabric
- sewing machine or needle and thread
- potpourri
- 3 yards ½" wide eggshell lace
- 8 round head pearl corsage pins, 2" long
- small silk flower cluster approx. 5" diameter in shades to match fabric
- green floral tape
- ⅛" satin ribbon, 3 yards French blue and 1¼ yards rose mauve
- 8 small pink silk flowers

1. Using 5 yards of moire ribbon, wrap wreath and secure ends of ribbon with glue. Wrap 3 yards of lace ribbon over moire ribbon. Secure ends with glue. Make wreath hanger from 8" of wire (see page 8); attach to wreath.

2. Using 2 yards of lace ribbon, make ½" pleats and staple. Space pleats approximately an inch apart. Attach pleated ribbon to back edge of wreath with glue.

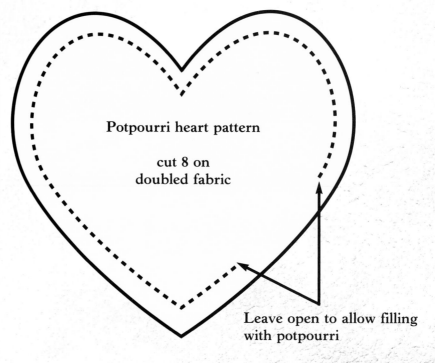

Potpourri heart pattern

cut 8 on
doubled fabric

Leave open to allow filling with potpourri

Stitch on dotted line

3. Use remaining lace ribbon to make 6 loop bow (about 9" wide, with 8" streamers). No center loop is added to this bow. Attach bow to wreath with glue.

4. Trace heart pattern onto tracing paper with pencil. Cut out and use heart as a pattern piece. Double fabric and cut out 8 hearts.

5. With wrong sides together, stitch around heart ½" from edge; leave 2" unstitched. Fill hearts with 1½ to 2 tablespoons of potpourri. Stitch heart closed and trim edges ¼" from stitching. Glue lace ruffle on top of stitching on front side of heart. Make 8 hearts.

6. Place corsage pin through center of heart and pin to wreath.

7. Make 5" cluster of silk flowers and tape stems together with floral tape. Using 1¼ yards each of French blue and rose-mauve satin ribbon together, make 16 loop bow (4" wide, with 4" to 5" streamers). Wire bow to stem of flower cluster. Glue cluster to center of bow.

8. Make 8 small shoestring bows from blue satin ribbon. Glue small pink flower onto center of each bow. Glue a bow to each heart.

BRAIDED BREAD DOUGH WREATH

This is truly an easy wreath to make, though it looks like quite the chore! In fact, they are so easy you'll want to make some for your friends. A bread wreath is a homey decoration and reminds us of the mouth-watering aroma and warmth that fills the home when bread bakes in the oven.

1. Spray pizza pan with cooking spray, place frozen loaves on pan and allow to defrost and rise until double. Sprinkle flour on working surface, and stretch each loaf until it is 36" long. Lay pieces side by side and braid. Lay braided piece around inside edge of pan, overlapping ends slightly. Spray braid with cooking spray. Let rise until double.

2. Bake in oven, usually 350° for 25 to 30 minutes or until golden brown. Remove bread from oven, reduce temperature of oven to 150°. Let bread cool until you can handle it. Transfer it to a cooling rack and place into 150° oven and leave bread in oven with door ajar for 24 to 30 hours. Bread must be very hard and dry. Remove bread from oven and allow to cool.

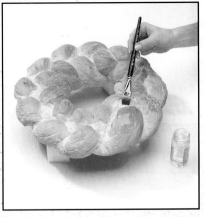

3. Spread nonstick paper onto working surface. When wreath is cool, place on prepared surface and spray with clear acrylic sealer spray to seal the bread. Let dry. Elevate wreath so drips will fall on nonstick paper. Brush on one coat of high gloss finish, coating top of wreath, let dry, then coat bottom, watching for drips. Repeat coating. This step seals the wreath and protects it from moisture and mold. Let dry.

Materials

- 14" pizza pan
- cooking spray
- 1 pkg. of 3 frozen loaves of bread dough
- bread board or waxed paper
- flour
- oven
- cooling rack
- nonstick paper
- clear acrylic sealer spray, matte
- 2 bottles high gloss finish
- 1" soft bristled brush
- 28-gauge white covered wire
- 2 silk daisy sprays
- 8 sprigs black bearded wheat
- wire cutters
- ruler
- glue gun and glue sticks
- floral tape, green
- 1 yard wired paper twist, natural
- 3 yards blue check ribbon
- scissors

4. Cluster several daisy sprays together and add 4 wheat stalks. Wire stems together. Make two clusters. Each cluster should measure about 10". Overlap stems of flower clusters, with flowers pointing in opposite directions, and wire together. Cover wired area with floral tape. Apply glue to taped area of cluster and glue to wreath over joined section of bread.

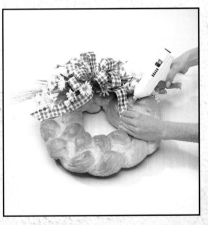

5. Fold wired paper twist in half and twist together 1" from fold. Place loop in back of wreath and bring ends around to front over flower stems and twist together. This forms the hanger and also helps secure the flowers (see page 8). Make a 10 loop bow (8" wide, with 10" streamers). Glue bow over center of flowers. Drape streamers to sides and glue to wreath. If needed, glue several extra daisies and leaves above and below bow to cover hanger and bow wire.

SIMPLY ELEGANT
LACE HEART WREATH

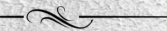

Simple elegance describes this lovely wreath made from printed
ruffled lace. Embellish your treasure with pearls and flowers and
recreate the beauty of days gone by.

Materials

- 11" plastic foam heart
- wire cutters
- 6" 16-gauge wire
- glue gun and glue sticks
- pointed metal nail file
- tape measure
- 11 yards 2½" mauve/blue printed ruffled lace
- scissors
- 1 yard 1" white nylon ruffled lace trim
- 1⅔ yard string of 4mm white pearl beads
- 5 2" wired green cloth rose leaves
- green floral tape
- dressmaker's pin
- 2⅔ yards mauve moire ribbon
- 6" 32-gauge green cloth-covered wire
- 5 mauve silk rosebuds, ½"

1. Make a wire loop hanger (see page 8) and glue it to the upper back of the wreath. With the nail file point, push (tuck) the lace into the foam in six continuous rows. Make sure right side of lace is up. Begin with the outside row and go counterclockwise from the center top, leaving ½" of the foam on the back of the heart exposed. Move the file over 1", catch the lace in the point, back up ¼" and push the lace in until it is taut. Be sure not to pull the previous tuck out.

2. When you complete the first row at the center top, move over and continue in the same direction for the second row without cutting the lace. Tuck close to the first row to avoid gaps. In the same manner, complete a total of five rows, ending at the center top. Continue in the same direction for the sixth and final row on the inside center of the wreath. Position the row leaving ½" of foam on the back of the heart exposed as in Step 1. End the tucking at the center top of the heart by cutting the lace and leaving enough to make the final tuck at the center top *V*.

3. To conceal the visible foam in the center of the wreath, glue the 1" white lace overlapping the tucked lace about 1/16". Begin and end at the bottom point. View the wreath from all angles. If gaps between the rows reveal foam or if the lace doesn't fall properly, spot glue sparingly near the foam to hold the lace in place.

4. Glue one row of pearls on the inside center where the wide and narrow laces meet. Make them visible from the front. Stack five leaves evenly with right sides up. With floral tape, secure the stems together beginning ½" from the bottom of the leaves. Spread the leaves in a fan shape and glue to the center top. Push a dressmaker's pin through the leaf cluster while glue is still warm to secure cluster.

5. From the ribbon and remaining pearls, make a simple bow. Make two looped streamers and two bow loops on each side of center. Add the pearls in the same manner, making one looped strand on each side. Crimp the ribbon and pearls together in the center and tie with 32-gauge wire. Glue the wired portion at the base of the leaves. Glue a tight cluster of five rosebuds to the leaves above the bow.

BEAUTIFUL BRIDE WREATH

Delicate silk flowers made into a head wreath with a gathered tulle veil create a vision of sweet innocence and delicate charm. The crowning glory of your wedding ensemble will add the touch of perfection to your special day. How can anything be so lovely, easy to make, and still be so inexpensive?

1. Measure one strand of wire (18 gauge) around bride's head. Overlap wire 2" and cut. Add 2 more strands of wire of the same length and wrap onto circle with white floral tape. Wrap 1 yard of satin ribbon around the circle, over the floral tape. Glue ends of ribbon to the ring.

2. Cut two 3" lengths of wire (28 gauge) and make two small loops. Add to sides of ring by twisting ends around ring (for bobby pins or comb). Hold wreath in both hands between the wire loops. Bend circle downward slightly. This will help the wreath conform to the shape of the head.

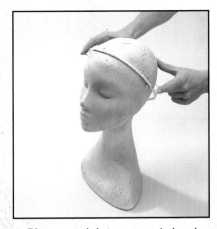

3. Place wreath base onto wig head form. (Note: You can also use an inverted mixing bowl.) Use several floral pins to hold the headpiece in place on the wig head form.

Materials

- 3 36" lengths 18-gauge white-covered wire or 6 18" lengths
- wire cutters
- white floral tape
- 1½ yards satin ribbon, eggshell
- glue gun and glue sticks
- scissors
- 28-gauge white-covered wire
- wig head form
- floral pins
- bleached, preserved galaxy gypsophila (gyp)
- 12 silk dried-look mini rosebuds, candlelight
- 1 silk gypsophila (gyp) blossom spray, candlelight
- 12 silk dried-look larkspur, soft white
- 1 silk dried-look hydrangea, blush
- eggshell tulle, 108" wide, desired length (optional)

4. Cut flowers apart, leaving 1" stems. Break gyp into short sprigs. Arrange flowers into separate piles. Beginning at the back of the wreath, put an inch strip of glue to wire and lay sprigs of gyp, rose bud, silk gyp blossoms, and hydrangea blossom. Repeat process until you work your way completely around wreath. You can add the veil in step 5 or stop here.

5. Lay out doubled veil material (measured for desired length) on cutting pad or cardboard. Using rotary cutter, cut away corner on open end of veil. Open up veil and stitch across straight edge of veil to gather. Pull gathers to desired fullness, cover top of veil with remaining eggshell ribbon, and stitch across to secure. Apply hot glue to underside of back of wreath. Lay gathered end of veil into glue and press firmly. (Note: If you get glue on veil, place it between two pieces of paper towel and press with iron. Glue will be absorbed into paper towel.)

SOUTHWESTERN
CHILI PEPPER WREATH

Add a little "zest" to your southwest kitchen decor with sprays of brilliant red chili peppers clustered on a straw wreath base. Raffia bows between the peppers and a multilooped paper-jute bow enhance this festive wreath.

Materials

- 14" straw wreath
- about 64 strands natural raffia (18" long)
- 2 strings of artificial red chili peppers or about 18 clusters (3 peppers per cluster)
- scissors
- tacky glue
- floral pins
- 28-gauge floral wire for bow
- 3 yards paper-jute ribbon

1. Using several strands of raffia, make chenille stem hanger (see page 8). Tie raffia hanger around straw wreath.

2. Remove chili pepper clusters from string and attach clusters to wreath with floral pins hooked over stem of chili peppers. Dip floral pins into glue before inserting into wreath. Direct peppers downward from each side of wreath center.

3. Cluster three or four 18" strands of raffia together and shape into bow. Place floral pin over center of bow and push pin into wreath. Place approximately 12 bows throughout clusters of chili peppers. Trim streamers that are too long.

4. Using paper-jute ribbon, make 12 loop bow (6" wide, with 10" streamers). Apply glue to back of bow and place bow at center top of wreath. Bring bow wires to back of wreath and twist ends together. Trim excess wire. Drape bow streamers to each side of wreath and hold in place with floral pin.

FRUIT & IVY
COUNTRY WREATH

Create this vibrant wreath to brighten your kitchen or family room. Perhaps you might change the colors by substituting a fabric ribbon of your choice with coordinated paper ribbon and fruit. By making changes to suit your taste, the wreath will become uniquely yours.

Materials

- 12" heart straw wreath
- 6" 16-gauge wire
- low temperature glue gun and glue sticks
- scissors
- tape measure
- 4½ yards red paper twist
- 26 floral pins
- 4 yards red/white gingham ribbon
- 15 6" ivy vines (2" leaves or smaller)
- wire cutters
- 3 40mm red lacquered apples
- 24 15mm wired lacquered berries
- 24 10 mm wired lacquered berries
- green floral tape

1. Make a wire loop hanger (see page 8) and glue it to the upper back. Trim the stray ends of straw. Cut, untwist, and spread a 7½-foot length of paper twist. Fold evenly in half lengthwise and cut along the fold. Set one strip aside. Spiral the other evenly around the wreath, beginning and ending on the back at the bottom point. Bring the ends together with a floral pin. Spiral a 7½-foot strip of ribbon over the paper ribbon.

2. Make a French bow (see page 9) of gingham and paper twist. Gingham ribbon is not added to the streamer. Glue the bow and streamer to the top of the wreath. With floral pins, secure four 6" ivy vines to each side of the wreath, overlapping them to converge at the bottom point of the heart. Direct the stem ends toward the bottom point, covering stems with the leaves of the next vine. Cut the stems from two more 6" ivy vines and cross them in an inverted V. Attach with floral pins to the bottom point, with ends falling below the point.

3. Glue a cluster of the three large apples nestled among the leaves at the bottom point. Separate 10mm berries into eight groups with three berries in each. Cluster the three berries together and stretch and wrap floral tape on 2" of the stems; cut excess wire. Make eight clusters of 10mm berries and eight clusters of 15mm berries. Randomly glue four clusters of each size on each side of the heart; tuck stems under leaves.

4. Glue two 6" ivy vines above the bow, concealing glued portions under the bow. Cut apart the remaining ivy and glue individual leaves as needed to conceal floral pins and berry cluster stems.

CANDLE RING OF DRIED FLOWERS

Create a cozy atmosphere for entertaining or add a homey touch to everyday living with this beautiful dried-flower candle ring. Cover a straw wreath with Spanish moss and glue dried flowers and pine cones to the ring. When finished, you'll have a project to be proud of.

1. Cover the wreath with Spanish moss and attach with floral pins. Then wrap loosely with monofilament line. Do not trim the stray ends of moss.

2. Place the hurricane globe in the center of the ring. Prepare the dried materials to glue at random to the Spanish moss. Distribute them evenly for variety and color. Place them from close to the globe to table level. If necessary, remove the stems from the straw flowers before gluing both colors at random to the moss. Leave 1" stems on the statice sinuata. Tuck the glued stems under the moss, making about five large clusters that will give a mass of color. Glue them at different levels and angles.

3. Leave short stems on the yarrow and cockscomb. If the blossoms are large, break them apart into 2" flower heads. If they are small, cluster and glue them into 2" flowers. Add the globe amaranth on stems from 1" to 3". Place them in clusters at all levels and angles. Glue the stem ends of the spruce cones at all levels and angles.

Materials

- 10" straw wreath
- 5 oz. Spanish moss
- 24 floral pins
- 5 yards monofilament fishing line or gray thread
- low temperature glue gun and glue sticks
- scissors
- tape measure
- 9" pillar candle, color of your choice
- 12" hurricane globe
- straw flowers: 12 cream and 12 cranberry
- 1 oz. purple statice sinuata
- 2 oz. natural dried yarrow
- 5 2" diameter cranberry cockscomb blossoms
- 65 mauve dried globe amaranth blossoms on natural stems
- 12 white spruce cones (or similar variety)
- 2 oz. natural dried caspia
- surface sealer spray

4. To give airiness to the ring, break off 2" and 3" caspia tips. Tuck the glued stems into the moss between the flowers. Place them at various angles, using their wispy tips to advantage. View the ring from all angles. If necessary, add leftover dried materials to conceal visible glue. Add additional materials to cascade onto the table if needed.

5. In a well-ventilated area, spray the dried materials to help prevent shattering.

CINNAMON APPLE WREATH

A cinnamon stick wreath creates a background for preserved apple slices. A perky bow of crisp windowpane plaid and a decorated wooden spoon accent this kitchen wreath that evokes the delicious, fragrant aroma of fresh baked apple pie.

Materials

- 10" × 2" cardboard or wood ring
- chenille stem for hanger
- approx. 90 cinnamon sticks, 3" to 4" long
- tacky glue (glue gun will not hold cinnamon onto wreath)
- craft stick or glue brush
- 10 preserved apple slices
- 2 yards windowpane plaid ribbon
- 28-gauge floral wire
- wooden spoon, 12" long (If you paint apple onto spoon bowl you will also need acrylic paints: country red, leaf green, ebony, and snow white; ¼" flat brush and liner brush; water; paper towels.)

Recipe
for preserving apple slices

2 cups lemon juice
1 tablespoon salt
large mixing bowl
5 or 6 apples
cutting board
sharp knife
screen or cooling rack
clear acrylic sealer spray

Directions:
1. Mix lemon juice and salt together in mixing bowl.
2. Cut apples into ¼" thick slices.
3. Soak apple slices in lemon juice mixture for 3 minutes.
4. Lay slices on screen or cooling rack and place in 150° oven for 5 to 6 hours or until slices begin to curl and feel leathery. LEAVE OVEN DOOR AJAR.
5. Allow slices to cool, then spray both sides of each slice with a clear acrylic spray.
Note: Treated apple slices may vary in color and will darken over time.

1. Attach chenille stem to top of wreath to form hanger (see page 8). Spread tacky glue over wreath base with craft stick or glue brush and lay cinnamon sticks side by side. You may have to layer sticks in some areas to cover cardboard base.

2. Apply glue to back of apple slices and lay 5 slices down each side of wreath, over cinnamon sticks.

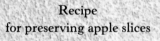

3. Make a 10 loop bow (6" wide, with 5" streamers). Apply glue to back of bow and place bow at top of wreath between apple slices. Bring bow wire to back of wreath and twist ends together. Trim away excess wire.

4. Apply glue to back of the top of the spoon handle and to bowl. Place handle into bow loop and bowl of spoon at bottom of wreath. (Spoon may be decorated with a small apple painted on bowl of spoon.)

Blue jeans and eyelet-trimmed dresses represent the back-to-school theme for this novelty wreath. Whether you make it for your home or as a gift for your child's teacher, there is a touch of nostalgia in it for everyone. The accessories here are for the young student. If an older child is the subject of your theme, select appropriate materials and add your own blackboard message.

Materials

- 14" round straw wreath
- 6" 16-gauge wire
- wire cutters
- low temperature glue gun and glue sticks
- scissors
- tape measure
- 4¼ yards blue paper twist
- floral pins
- 2 yards ¾" white ruffled eyelet
- one piece chalk
- 5" × 7" blackboard
- 2 2" diameter red lacquered apples
- 3 2" × 3" blackboards
- School supplies (one of each): blue pencil, 6" red ruler, red pencil sharpener, red crayon, blue crayon, blunt scissors

1. Make a wire loop hanger (see page 8) and glue it to the upper back of the wreath. Trim the stray ends of straw from the wreath.

2. Cut off 64" of paper twist. Untwist but don't spread it to its full width. Spiral it evenly around the wreath and bring the ends together on the back; secure with a floral pin. In the same manner, spiral the same amount of eyelet at the edge of the paper ribbon; secure with a floral pin.

3. Make a French bow (see page 9) from the paper twist. Glue it to the bottom middle of the wreath. With chalk, write your message on the blackboard and glue it to the left inside edge of the wreath. Make sure no glue is visible. Glue two apples above the bow, at different angles.

4. To one mini blackboard, glue a pencil, ruler, and sharpener at different angles. To the second, glue two crayons. To the third, glue the opened scissors. Glue the blackboards evenly around the wreath.

5. Face: Nose–cut 5" length of aqua paper twist. Fold in half lengthwise, then in half again. Fold length of the piece in half and twist in center, gluing the two halves together. Fold ¾" from end. Apply glue to folded end and attach to center of face. Cut out two ⅝" circles from index card. Outline circle with black permanent marker and fill in eye leaving white crescent to right side of eye (see pattern). Glue eyes to face just above nose. Draw small crescent for mouth.

6. Hair: Cut three 21" lengths of metallic purple twist. Cut ½" wide slits in each piece. Using a floral pin, pin strips on head to form hair. Trim ends.

7. Hat: Fold black felt square in half across the 12" length. Measure 6" from the folded corner and mark with straight pins (see diagram). Cut along pin line. Form piece into cone and glue overlapping edges together. Cut brim from curve in felt, with center measuring 2" and taper off to point on each end (see diagram). Slash curve of brim ½" along inside edge. Apply glue to slashes and attach to underside of crown, bringing tapered ends to back of hat. Trim hat with orange satin ribbon. Pin hat to head with straight pins.

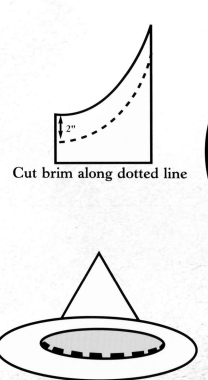

Cut along pin line

8. Make a 6 loop bow from Halloween ribbon (6" wide, with 5" streamers) and glue to witch's neck. Glue broom into witch's hand.

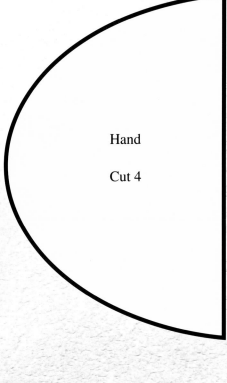

Hand

Cut 4

Cut brim along dotted line

Eyes

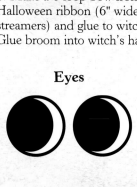

Glue slashes to inside of crown

AUTUMN GLOW WREATH

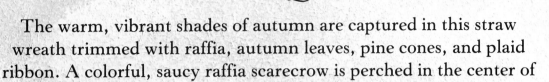

The warm, vibrant shades of autumn are captured in this straw wreath trimmed with raffia, autumn leaves, pine cones, and plaid ribbon. A colorful, saucy raffia scarecrow is perched in the center of the wreath to give a friendly welcome to all.

AUTUMN GLOW WREATH

Materials

- 18" straw wreath
- 12 oz. pkg. of natural raffia
- floral pins
- 6 yards ribbon, autumn tones
- scissors
- 28-gauge floral wire
- wire cutters
- preserved fall leaves
- tacky glue
- 8 pine cones, 4" long
- 18-gauge wire
- 12" wood dowel stick, ¼"
- 3" foam ball
- ruler
- 2 12mm solid black doll eyes
- black permanent marking pen
- 12" × 15" orange burlap
- needle and thread
- gold felt square for patches
- 1 yard green velvet ribbon
- 1 orange feather, 4" long
- 6" straw hat

1. Unwrap wreath if wrapped in plastic. Attach several strands of raffia to wreath for hanger according to chenille stem hanger instructions (see page 8). Straighten out raffia strands. Keep all strands tied together in center. Pull off 12 to 15 strands of raffia and tie them around the wreath in a bow, securing with a floral pin. Repeat 3 more times, placing tied raffia in four places around wreath, equal distances apart.

2. Cut 2⅓ yards of ribbon and starting at top back, loop ribbon on top of the wreath. Attach ribbon to wreath with floral pins. With remaining ribbon, make a 12 loop bow (9" wide, with 6" streamers). Attach bow to top of wreath by wrapping bow wire around wreath and twisting ends together in back of wreath. Trim excess wire.

3. Open package of fall leaves and cut branches apart into shorter stems. Glue branches into straw around wreath. Attach 9" of wire to each pine cone, leaving a 3" wire stem. Dip wire stem into glue and place pine cone into wreath, nestled in leaves and raffia.

4. Scarecrow: Dip end of wood dowel into glue and push into foam ball. Using about 60 strands of raffia, fold raffia strands in half and tie together in center with strand of raffia. Center tied area of raffia over foam ball and pull strands smooth over ball and tie together at base of ball around dowel stick. Measure down 18" from top of ball and cut off excess raffia.

5. Use long cut-off strands of raffia to form arms. Tie the center of this cluster with strands of raffia. Arms should measure about 20" long. Place arm between raffia strands, beneath head. Tie all strands together beneath arms, forming waist. Divide strands below waist into two equal sections and tie ends together to form legs. Tie ends of arms together.

6. Hair: Tie a cluster of 10" strands of raffia together in center and pin to top of head. Glue black eyes to face by pushing glue coated shanks into foam. Draw crescent mouth with black permanent marker.

7. Jacket: Fold 15" length of orange burlap in half, then fold again in opposite direction. Following diagram, cut out jacket. Slit one fold for front opening. Hand sew side seams together (you may also staple seams); turn to right side. Cut out two gold felt patches. Glue patches to jacket with tacky glue. Make stitch marks with black permanent marker. Put jacket on scarecrow. Tie shoestring bow with ½ yard velvet ribbon and glue to neck.

8. Trim hat with green velvet ribbon and feather. Attach to head with several floral pins. Dip end of dowel stick into glue and push down into wreath to sit scarecrow in wreath.

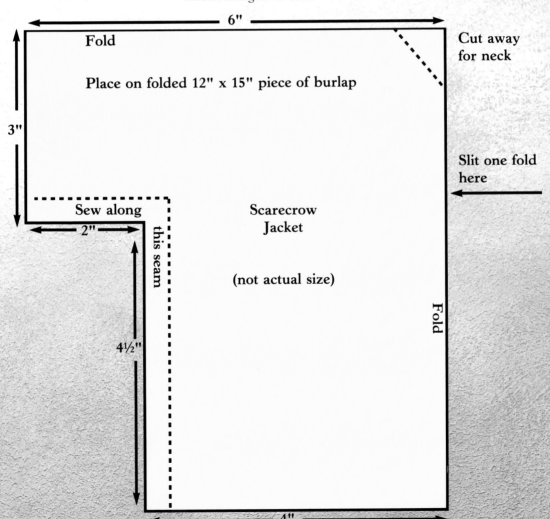

VICTORIAN WREATH

The glitz of the Victorian era is reflected in this lamé-wrapped wreath
of evergreens, silk roses, and golden walnuts. You'll discover, as the
Victorians did, that gold blends well with holiday decorating.

Materials

- 12" plastic-wrapped heart straw wreath
- 6 yards lamé metallic gold ribbon, 2½"
- scissors
- floral pins
- 6" 16-gauge wire
- low temperature glue gun and glue sticks
- wire cutters
- 30 5" sprigs artificial evergreens,
  some cut to 4" and 3"
- 7 English walnuts
- small pointed knife
- metallic spray, brilliant gold
- aluminum pie pan
- 1⅓ yards red/green/metallic striped ⅜"
  ribbon
- tape measure
- red silk roses with leaves: 4 2" blossoms
  with 2 buds; 6 sets of 3 rose leaf clusters

1. Spiral wrap the wreath with lamé ribbon, beginning and ending on the center top of the wreath on the front (covered later with greens). Secure both ends with floral pins. Make a wire loop hanger (see page 8) and glue to the upper back.

2. NOTE: The evergreen needles fall in one direction on each wire stem. Attach them to the wreath in the same direction. With floral pins, secure one end of 12 5" evergreen sprigs to the wreath on the left side beginning halfway up the wreath and ending at the center top. Position them in pairs in an inverted V pattern as you work up toward the center. Repeat on the opposite side. Adjust greens and trim the ends if too long.

3. Carefully pry open walnuts and remove nuts; glue the matching halves back together. In a well-ventilated area, spray them with fast-drying metallic gold paint. Place them in the aluminum pan and turn as needed to coat completely. From striped ribbon, cut three hangers: 14", 16", and 18". Glue the ends together and glue one walnut to the bottom of each looped ribbon. Glue the ends in a cluster and hang from the bottom point.

4. To conceal the ribbon ends of the hanging walnuts, glue two 4" evergreens (needles facing opposite directions) in a V. Glue two 3" sprigs beneath them in the same manner, but in an inverted V with all four stems converging at the point. Cut one 5" evergreen in half. Turn one piece around and glue them in an inverted V at the center top of the heart where the stems converge. Position them to be seen below the point.

5. Cut roses and leaves from stems. Glue three roses in a cluster in the center top and one at the bottom of the heart where greens converge. Glue one three-leaf cluster horizontally on each side of the upper roses and one on each side of the lower rose. Conceal the glued stems under the roses.

6. Glue a rosebud and one 3-leaf cluster on the left and right sides pointing down. Tuck the cut ends under the greens. Glue two walnuts among the greens on the upper left curve of the heart and two on the upper right curve. Conceal visible floral pins by gluing 1" sprigs of greens.

NATURAL ELEGANCE CHRISTMAS WREATH

Pods, cones, preserved citrus slices, and pine create an elegant decoration for the holiday season. A red velvet bow with cascading gold jingle bells will surely add elegance to your Christmas decor.

1. Shape wreath by pulling out and fluffing branches. (You may choose to use a natural wreath, which will probably not need fluffing.)

2. Make garland of pods with wire stems, using paddle wire. Garland should be long enough to fit around wreath. Use lotus, okra, poppy pods, bell cups, and protea in garland.

3. Lay garland on top of wreath and twist pine fronds over garland to hold in place. (If using fresh wreath, wire garland into wreath.)

Materials

- 27" to 30" artificial Colorado spruce wreath
- stemmed pods: 7 medium lotus pods, 8 okra pods, 9 poppy pods, 5 bell cups, 4 protea
- 28-gauge paddle wire
- rosebloom protea
- 2 clusters agave
- 2 bunches preserved pepperberries
- 1 bunch yarrow, gold
- 7 persevered citrus slices
- preserved baby breath, natural
- hot glue gun and glue sticks or tacky glue
- 3 yards wired red velvet ribbon
- 28-gauge floral wire
- scissors
- ruler
- 1½ yards red velvet cording
- 4 1½" diameter gold jingle bells
- wire cutters

4. Glue in stems of rosebloom protea, agave, pepperberries, yarrow, citrus slices, and preserved baby breath.

5. Using wired ribbon, make a 6 loop bow (10" wide, with 12" streamers). Tie bells to ends of two 24" lengths of red velvet cording. Catch cording into bow wire at back of bow, staggering the lengths of cords. Wire bow to top of wreath. Trim wire. Drape streamers to sides of wreath and secure with glue.

MUSICAL HOLIDAY WREATH

Holiday music brings fond memories back to us all. This musical wreath is a reflection of that nostalgia, from the vibrant velvet ribbon inscribed with gold music to the matching gold instruments.

1. Insert a chenille stem through the wire frame on the back of the wreath. Twist the ends together making a hanger loop (see page 8). With a craft stick or butter knife, frost all sides of the cones with snow texturizing, starting at the base of the cone and working toward the tip. Set aside on wax paper to dry.

2. Entwine the gold bead garland among the branches, allowing it to fall gracefully. Final adjustments will be made later. For the banner, cut a 22" length of ribbon. Tuck it among the branches from between center left to top, just right of center. Glue ribbon to the branches, and ripple the wire edges slightly. Following the instructions on page 10, make a multiloop bow (8" wide, with 12" streamers). Crumple the wire edges of the ribbon slightly to create a rippled bow. Glue it to the bottom right of the wreath.

3. Attach 6" lengths of metallic gold cord to the instruments as hangers. Position the instruments at random. Wrap each cord hanger around the bough twice, allowing each instrument to dangle. Adjust them for balance and variety. To make one berry cluster, bend three wired berries in half to make six berries per cluster. Stretch and wrap the floral tape around the wires. Make 12 more clusters. Glue their taped stems to the branches at random; conceal glue and tape under the branches.

Materials

- 16" artificial evergreen wreath
- 12" green chenille stem
- craft stick or butter knife
- 12 2" spruce cones
- snow texturizing
- small piece wax paper
- 2 yards 8mm gold strung bead garland
- 3⅓ yards red velvet/gold wire-edge music score ribbon
- tape measure
- scissors
- glue gun and glue sticks
- 28-gauge floral wire
- 2 yards fine metallic gold cord (to hang ornaments)
- 12 3" assorted gold plastic instruments
- 39 wired double-ended red berries
- green floral tape
- 5" white feathered dove
- wire cutters
- 1 yard 32-gauge green cloth-covered wire

4. Cut the wires from the dove's feet and glue it above the banner at the top. Adjust the gold beads and secure them to the branches in about ten spots by twisting 2" lengths of green 32-gauge wire around them. When the cones have dried, glue them at random among the branches, tilting them at various angles.

PINE CONE WREATH

Enjoy the natural beauty of pine cones year after year with this lovely holiday wreath. Once you've mastered the technique, change the cone selection and pattern to create a unique gift.

1. Soak the Norway spruce cones in water for two hours or until they close. Drain on newspapers. Curved side of the frame is the top, which is the front of the wreath. Wedge the stem end of the wet cones compactly between the two upper and two lower wires. Fill wreath with cones. Insert the chenille stem through the wires on the back and twist into a loop for a hanger. Hang to dry.

2. The dry cones open again and create a tight base for the wreath. Wear gloves to protect your hands from sharp cones. Set aside seven large sweet gum balls for Step 5. With wire cutters, remove stems from the remaining sweet gum balls. Then glue two compact rows to the stem end of the spruce cones in the center of the wreath, concealing the wires. After gluing, hold each for a few seconds until it adheres. In a compact circle, glue the scotch cones close to the sweet gum balls. Glue half of the hemlock cones in the spaces between the sweet gum balls.

3. Glue the stem end of the 5" white pine cones in a circle wedged between the scotch cones added in Step 2. Position them in the same direction as the bottom cone layer (like the spokes of a wheel). View the wreath from the side and note the space between the two layers of cones. Wedge in and glue the 4" white pine cones to fill spaces. Glue the remaining hemlock cones in the spaces around the scotch cones and around the stems of the white pine.

Materials

- Cones and pods: (approx.) 35 6" Norway spruce cones; 35 5" and 24 4" white pine cones; 65 sweet gum balls; 30 scotch (or banks) cones; 200 hemlock cones
- pail of water
- 14" wire box wreath frame
- 12" brown chenille stem
- gardening gloves
- wire cutters
- glue gun and glue sticks
- tape measure
- floral sprays: glossy wood tone and brilliant gold
- 2 4½" red feathered cardinals
- 3 yards red velvet craft ribbon, 2½"
- scissors
- 6" 32-gauge green cloth-covered wire
- 39 6mm wired, double-ended holly berries
- brown floral tape

4. In a well-ventilated area, coat the wreath with glossy wood spray. Hold each of seven sweet gum balls by its stem and spray with brilliant gold. Cut off the stems and set aside. Glue the two cardinals to the top of the wreath facing each other. Make a multiloop bow (see page 10), which measures 10" wide with 3" loops on each side and with 12" and 14" streamers. Secure gathers with 32-gauge wire. Glue bow to the wreath at the center bottom.

5. To make a berry cluster, bend three wired berries in half to make six berries per cluster. Stretch and wrap the floral tape around the wires. Make 12 more clusters. Glue the taped berries, with the stems tucked between the cones, at random. Glue the 7 gold sweet gum balls to the wreath spaced evenly.

WILLIAMSBURG-INSPIRED
CHRISTMAS SWAG

Create this vibrant Williamsburg-inspired holiday swag in two hours or less. In the true Williamsburg tradition, fresh greens, fruits, and berries are used. To have more than one season's enjoyment, use preserved greens like those pictured. Display your creation on a sheltered entryway and its beauty will be admired by all.

Materials

- 3" × 4" corrugated cardboard
- tape measure
- scissors
- awl
- 12" green chenille stem
- low temperature glue gun and glue sticks
- 3" × 4" block dry floral foam
- serrated knife
- small garden clippers

- 1-pound bunch preserved cedar
- 2 8-oz. bunches preserved boxwood
- 1-pound bunch preserved black spruce
- 3 2½" floral picks
- 6 long stemmed natural dried yarrow with 3" to 4" diameter blossoms

- 3 red delicious artificial apples
- 9 12" lengths 18- or 20-gauge wire
- 81 10mm wire-stemmed lacquered berries
- green floral tape
- wire cutters
- white pine cones: 7 6"; 1 4"

1. Cut a 3" × 4" piece of corrugated cardboard. With an awl, puncture two evenly spaced holes in the cardboard, 1" down and parallel to one narrow end. Make a hanger by bending a 12" chenille stem into a *U*. Three inches down from the *U*, twist the stem into a 3" loop. Push the wire ends through the holes in the cardboard, pulling the twisted portion of the hanger tightly against the cardboard, twist ends, and press flat against the cardboard. Glue the twisted wire down and reinforce the connection of the chenille stem and the cardboard around the holes with glue.

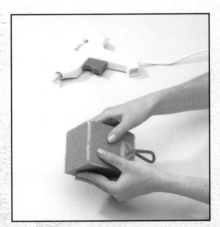

2. With cardboard as a guide and using a serrated knife, cut a foam block the size of the cardboard. Glue the cardboard to the foam block (with hanger on outside). For added reinforcement, place a beading of glue along the four edges where the foam and cardboard meet. Hold the cardboard against the foam until glue cools.

3. Insert all materials at an angle as though to converge in the center of the foam block. With garden clippers, cut three long branches of cedar: one 19" and two 15" long. Trim bottom 3" of side branches. Insert the long branch in the center extreme back of the foam, extending 16" straight up from the top of the foam block. Place the other two branches angled in a *V* in front of the first branch with one closer to the front than the other.

4. In the same manner, insert cedar branches on the bottom of the swag, with the longest extending about 16" down from the bottom of the foam. Cover the remaining surface of the foam with 4" sprigs of boxwood on the front and sides with longer ones toward the back, while creating a horizontal width of about 16".

5. Within the outside dimensions of the materials already placed, fill in with long and short branches of black spruce. Insert long ones in a fan shape at the top and bottom between the cedar branches and shorter ones horizontally to extend the width to about 20".

6. Add two or three 12" branches of boxwood in front of the upper cedar branches and the same number below.

7. Holding apple firmly, carefully puncture it with an awl. Make a hole on the bottom of the apple large enough to insert the square end of a floral pick. Remove wire from the pick and glue into the hole; hold pick steady until glue cools. Insert apples clustered in center.

8. Insert six yarrow blossoms (three above apples, three below) into the foam at various levels. The longest ones can extend about 10" from the center of the apple cluster. To each of nine 12" lengths of 18- or 20-gauge wire, attach nine wired berries with floral tape. Place the wired berry stems in a cluster parallel to the floral wire, permitting the berries to extend 1½" above the wire. Tape the berry clusters to the wires. Insert the clusters at random among the greens, permitting a group of three clusters to cascade beneath the apples, and the remaining ones evenly distributed throughout the swag.

9. Glue seven 6" cones among the outside branches around the design. Tuck the glued stem ends between the branches, but make the cones visible from the front. Glue one 4" cone tucked among the branches above the apples. View the swag from all sides and fill in gaps with remaining greens. Use short branches of spruce and cedar in the front to add variety. When the swag is hung, the branches should be flush against the wall to conceal the foam holder.